the guide to owning a
Cockatoo

Gayle Soucek

T.F.H. Publications, Inc.
One TFH Plaza
Third and Union Avenues
Neptune City, NJ 07753

Copyright © 2003 by T.F.H. Publications, Inc.

This book has been published with the intent to provide accurate and authoritative information in regard to the subject matter within. While every precaution has been taken in preparation of this book, the publisher and author assume no responsibility for errors or omissions. Neither is any liability assumed for damages resulting from the use of the information herein.

ISBN 0-7938-2209-2

www.tfh.com

Contents

Introduction to Cockatoos

When most people think of parrots, they visualize vividly colored gaudy birds in a lush tropical rainforest. Although that image certainly holds

Although several species of cockatoos are commonly kept as pets, there are some populations that are threatened in the wild.

true of many parrot species, the members of the family Cacatuidae are mostly white or black (except for a very few gray or pink types), and they are just as likely to be found in grassy savannas, agricultural areas, arid scrub forests, and open woodlands. There are approximately 20 species of cockatoos, although the number varies depending on the authority quoted. Taxonomists and ornithologists frequently disagree on classifications, so a bird might be listed in one source as a separate species and in another as a sub-species.

There are, however, a few characteristics that are unique to all cockatoos and that distinguish them from their parrot brethren. For starters, cockatoos have erectile crests of feathers on their heads, which they display to indicate anger, excitement, or fear. These crests range from the small, barely

All cockatoos share the common trait of a crest of feathers, with varying degrees of length and color.

noticeable white crest on the Goffin's (*Cacatua goffini*), to the dramatic red and yellow striped crest of the Leadbeater's (*Cacatua leadbeateri*, also known as Major Mitchell's cockatoo). Cockatoos also have the ability to pull forward their cheek feathers, covering most or all of their lower beak. This cheek-puffing behavior usually indicates contentment, although it can be a sign that the bird is cold or sleepy.

As mentioned earlier, most cockatoos are either mostly white or mostly black. The black cockatoos include the genera *Calyptorhynchus* (found throughout Australia) and *Probosciger*, which inhabits New Guinea and a few surrounding islands. All of the black cockatoos are extremely rare in American aviculture and almost unheard of in the pet trade. Black Palm cockatoos (*Probosciger aterrimus*) are occasionally available, but at prices up to $20,000, these are hardly common pets. There are two species of gray cockatoos, the Gang-Gang (*Callocephalon fimbriatum*) and the Galah (*Eolophus roseicappilus*, also known as the Rose-breasted cockatoo). Gang-Gangs are rare and not really available in the United States. Galahs are sometimes available, but they are very pricey and prone to fatty tumors unless their diet is carefully monitored. In general, with the possible exception of the Galah, none of the black or gray cockatoos should be kept as pets, because they are all endangered and belong in captive-breeding programs.

One very common member of the cockatoo family is the cockatiel

Cockatiels are considered by most to be part of the cockatoo family, but they are generally treated as a different breed.

The majority of cockatoos are either mostly black or mostly white; the Black Palm cockatoo is rare and not generally kept as a pet.

Nymphicus hollandicus [Editor's note: This classification, although the opinion of many scientists and aviculturists, is still disputed by some who believe the cockatiel is a separate breed]. These small, long-tailed birds now come in a wide variety of colors due to mutations and selective breeding in captivity, but wild cockatiels are primarily gray with white and yellow markings. Though true members of the cockatoo family, they are quite different from their larger cousins in appearance, behavior, and care requirements, and they are usually treated in the pet trade as an entire-

ly separate breed. Because of these differences, and because many excellent books specifically focused on cockatiels already exist, I've chosen to exclude them from the remainder of this text. For practical purposes, when I refer to "pet cockatoos," I'm focusing mainly on the various species of white cockatoos that are commonly available on the pet market.

White cockatoos all belong to the genus *Cacatua*. These species are found throughout Australia, New Guinea and surrounding islands, Indonesia, and part of the Philippines. Though many of these are critically endangered in the wild, due in part to deforestation and uncontrolled trapping in the 1970s and '80s, several of these species exist in large numbers in captivity. Although cockatoos aren't particularly easy to breed, some dedicated aviculturists have established breeding flocks that supply a steady flow of chicks into the pet trade. Most common are the Goffin's (*C. goffini*), Umbrella (*C. alba*), Moluccan (*C. moluccencis,* also known as the Salmon-crested), the Sulphur-crested (various subspecies of *C. galerita* and *C. sulphurea*), and the Bare-eyed (*C. sanguinea*). In general, I find the Moluccan and the Umbrella to be the most affectionate, yet the most demanding and emotional of the white cockatoos. Bare-eyed and Goffin's tend to be mischievous and slightly more independent. Of course, these are just general-

The Sulphur-crested cockatoo, with its bright yellow crest of feathers, is among the most commonly kept cockatoos.

my Goffin's cockatoo breeder hens escaped from her flight cage in my basement aviary. Although we searched the bird room, we couldn't find her. A short while later, we heard a commotion in my husband's adjoining workshop. I crept in quietly, and there was the cockatoo, ecstatically playing with pliers and wrenches in a toolbox. I was able to catch her easily, because she attempted to fly away with a heavy wrench in her beak and couldn't gain altitude. The best toys for these birds are those that have moving parts that turn or disconnect. I give my cockatoos stainless steel bolts with a wing nut screwed on. The birds

izations, and individual birds can be quite different.

Cockatoos aren't known as prolific talkers, but most will learn to say a few words, and some develop a fairly good vocabulary. Where their intelligence really shines is in their mechanical ability. Although most parrots use their feet to hold food and other objects, many of the cockatoo species are highly dexterous and truly use their foot as a hand. They are superb at manipulating objects, and there are very few toys and cages that a cockatoo can't disassemble. Once, one of

A spectacular red and yellow striped crest characterizes the Leadbeater's cockatoo.

Cockatoos require a great deal of devotion, but they love to snuggle and will return 100 percent of your affection.

love to unscrew the nut, and a few even attempt to put the nut back on, although none have been successful yet.

Besides their mechanical ability, cockatoos are known for their loving nature. If there is one thing that is true of all cockatoos, it is this: they are extremely intelligent, affectionate, and demanding companions. An ignored or neglected cockatoo is perhaps one of the most pitiful creatures on earth. Although all parrots require affection and interaction, cockatoos seem unable to function without it. A neglected cockatoo will scream, pluck its feathers, and in extreme cases will mutilate its own flesh to the point of death. Noted parrot behaviorist Chris Davis once remarked that most cockatoos would prefer to be surgically grafted to their owner's bodies. Though this is perhaps a *slight* exaggeration, it does aptly describe the emotional neediness of these beautiful birds. Never buy a cockatoo unless you are committed to spending some quality time with it on a daily basis. If you cannot do so, I guarantee that both you and the bird will suffer.

Finding the Right Bird

Once you've decided that a cockatoo is the proper pet for your household, your next step is finding the right bird. This is a search that might take some time. Cockatoos and most other parrots have not been imported into this country since 1992, so the only young birds available are those that are born in captivity. Cockatoos are somewhat difficult to breed, so you might have to do a little research to find available birds.

PREVIOUSLY OWNED BIRDS

If this is your first large parrot, I strongly recommend that you stick with a young, handfed baby. Although there are plenty of older, previously owned cockatoos available through newspaper ads around the country, these are often problem birds that are being dumped by their owners because of behavioral troubles like feather pick-

ing, screaming, or biting. This is in no way the fault of the bird—most of these cockatoos were either poorly socialized as chicks or were purchased by an inexperienced or disinterested

It's a good idea to do some research before you buy a cockatoo, but it's even better to spend as much time as you can with different species.

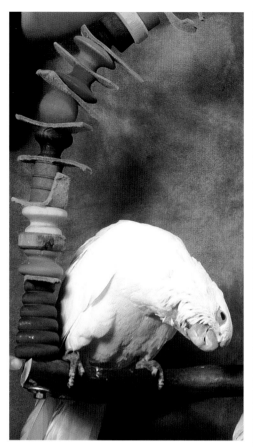

Birds of the same species can have different personalities, so it's important to know what kind of qualities suit your own character.

owner who was unable to provide the love, discipline, and structure that cockatoos require. In the hands of an experienced parrot person, many of these birds will blossom into wonderful companions, but they are most definitely not good candidates for a first bird household. There might be some perfectly delightful and well-behaved older cockatoos out there, but you won't have any real way of judging an older bird's pet potential until you live with it for awhile. Unfortunately, most people who are trying to unload an unwanted pet might "forget" to mention that its screams can peel the paint off the walls, or that they keep an economy-size box of bandages around the house for those nippy episodes. Your best bet for a tame loving pet is a recently weaned, handfed baby bird purchased from a pet shop or breeder.

PET SHOPS

Never purchase a bird (or any pet) on an impulse. Before you buy, you should carefully evaluate both the bird and the store itself. Are the cages clean? Is there a fresh and adequate supply of food and water? Are there toys in the cage? Do the shop personnel handle and interact with the birds, or are they shoved in a far corner and ignored? On the other hand, are the birds over-handled, stressed, and never allowed quiet time to rest? Is there a health guarantee? Have the larger parrots been vaccinated for viruses such as Polyomavirus?

These are all questions you'll want to consider before you make a decision. Some shops, especially those that specialize in parrots, will offer beautiful, loving, and healthy chicks. Other stores might have birds for sale, yet they are unprepared for or uneducated about the proper care of parrots, and you risk purchasing an unhealthy or poorly socialized bird. I recommend that you visit a store several times and get to know how they handle and care for animals before you make a final decision.

Once you're comfortable with the store, it's time to evaluate your potential new addition. Spend some time observing the birds. Cockatoo chicks are curious, intelligent, playful, and alert. Baby birds do nap frequently, but if a baby seems lethargic and doesn't show interest when you approach, it might be sick or depressed. Try visiting at another time and see how it acts then. A baby parrot should be friendly and approachable. Be wary of chicks that seem overly fearful or aggressive. Of course, even perfectly wonderful chicks can simply be having a bad day, or might be stressed, tired, or hungry, so don't give up after just one visit.

When approaching a baby parrot, speak softly and move slowly but confidently. Loud voices and abrupt fast movements can startle or frighten even the calmest chicks. On first visits, it's probably best to leave young children at home. Do not be concerned if a baby cockatoo hisses or raises its crest, unless it is showing other obvious signs of aggression or fear, such as biting or running away. Cockatoos use their crests to display many types of emotion, including excitement and happiness, as well as anger and fear. Some cockatoos will make hissing sounds and display their crests as a prelude to play. In other birds, this same behavior is a very serious threat posture. You will need to observe the bird for other signs to decide what is meant by the display. In general, a cockatoo that hisses or makes rapid clicking sounds with its beak while holding its wings close to its body and leaning forward is probably friendly and excited, while

Take time to study your cockatoo's body language. An erect crest may be a sign of happiness, excitement, fear, or aggression.

one that hisses, leans back, sways from side to side, and holds its wings open is most likely angry or afraid. If you're unsure, don't attempt to touch the bird, or you risk getting bitten. Ask the shop personnel about the behavior. Some babies will go into full threat posture just to see how you react, and then go back to playing a minute later. With a little observation and common sense, you'll soon be a pro at evaluating birdie body language.

PARROT BREEDERS

Another way to find a wonderful pet is by going straight to a cockatoo breeder. You can find listings of breeders in magazines like *Bird Talk*, *Bird Times*, or *Birds USA*. You also can check with any avian veterinarians or bird clubs in your area for referrals. Even if you don't find a parrot breeder that lists cockatoos, give some a call anyway. Unlike dog breeders, many parrot people raise numerous species, and they simply might not include them all in a small listing. Even if the person you speak to doesn't have cockatoos, they might be able to point you to a friend who does. The world of aviculture is a small, close-knit community, and most people will be happy to refer you to someone who breeds the species you're seeking.

Once you find a cockatoo breeder, you'll want to evaluate the person in much the same way as you looked at the pet stores. Look at how the baby birds are housed and fed. Understand that most breeders will not allow you to inspect the aviaries in which the

When checking out a breeder's facilities, look for healthy, energetic chicks and clean equipment and cages.

THE GUIDE TO OWNING A COCKATOO

A healthy cockatoo will have clear eyes, sleek feathers, and a smooth beak; always ask about health guarantees before making any purchase.

The Bare-eyed cockatoo, with its pale blue skin surrounding the eye, is relatively uncommon in the pet trade.

adult birds are kept. Although it's common in dog breeding to meet the puppy's parents and look over the kennels, birds are quite different. To an untamed breeding bird, strangers are potential predators that have come to wreak havoc and threaten their territory. The resultant stress is enough to make many birds desert their nests or kill their chicks. The risk of disease transmission is also high, so most aviaries are strictly off-limits to visitors. Of course, some small hobbyists might have just a few relatively tame breeding pairs in their living room; in any case, respect the breeder's policies, because they are acting in the best interest of their birds. Don't be afraid to ask questions. If possible, make a list beforehand and take it with you. Raising parrots is a labor of love, and most people who sell baby birds want very much to insure that their chicks end up in good homes. They'll usually be happy to dispense advice, tips, and other words of wisdom to help you care for your new pet.

BIRD FAIRS
Another place to find baby cockatoos is at a bird fair. These crop up in many communities, often during spring or fall months. Although they're most often hosted by local not-for-profit bird

clubs, some are scheduled on a regular basis by professional exhibition companies. These fairs give breeders and bird supply manufacturers an opportunity to reach the public in a flea market atmosphere. If you decide to buy a bird at one of these fairs, keep in mind a few cautions.

First of all, be certain that you know how to contact the seller after the fair. Although it's rare, there have been incidences of disreputable individuals who use these events to dump sick animals and then disappear. Ask for references. Often, the vendors will know each other and can vouch for the reputation of other sellers. If you have any doubts about the person or about the birds they're selling, walk away. You don't need the heartbreak and financial distress of purchasing a sick baby parrot.

Secondly, be aware that even healthy birds run a much higher risk of developing disease when exposed to others at a fair. Many avian diseases are hard to detect and easy to transmit, so one sick bird can endanger a whole exhibition hall full of healthy birds. If someone touches a sick bird (or its cage), then goes down the aisle touching other birds, they can spread the disease throughout the room. Unfortunately, you won't have any way of knowing that your new pet has been exposed until the illness strikes, which is often several days or even weeks later. Never buy a bird from someone who allows people to handle the chicks without first washing their hands or using an alcohol-based hand sanitizer.

UNWEANED CHICKS

Another issue you must consider is the age of the baby cockatoo you're considering purchasing. Many breeders and shops will only sell chicks that are fully weaned and able to eat on their own. Cockatoo chicks, like all other parrots, are altricial, which means they're born blind, naked, and helpless, and must be fed around the clock by either the parent birds or a human "nanny." In general, cockatoos wean between 12 to 24 weeks, depending on the species and the individual chick's temperament. There are also some people who sell unweaned young chicks that must still be handfed by humans. These folks claim that

To prevent the spread of disease to any birds you already have in your home, quarantine a new bird for a period of at least 30 days.

Cockatoos can be real clowns; sit back and enjoy your new bird's antics and playful behavior.

handfeeding such a young chick insures that the chick will bond to you. My personal feeling is that this is nonsense. Cockatoos are very loving and social creatures, and a healthy, properly socialized bird will bond to a new owner at any age. Buying an unweaned chick is a recipe for disaster.

First of all, handfeeding is an art that takes a great deal of skill and experience. If you feed the baby too fast, it can aspirate food and die. Feed too slow, and the chick might grow frustrated and stop eating. If the food is too hot, it can cause a serious crop burn, which is potentially lethal. Too cold, and the chick might refuse to eat or have difficulty digesting the formula. Even highly experienced breeders can lose babies due to errors in handfeeding, but at least they might have the

knowledge to respond properly should an emergency arise. Feeding parrot chicks is not an easy task for beginners. Yes, you can learn, but you are not doing yourself or the chick any favors by taking the risk. I've seen far too many beautiful young parrots killed or injured by well-meaning but inexperienced new owners who are bullied into taking unweaned chicks by breeders and stores that insist it's the best way to bond with the bird.

Secondly, cockatoos are notoriously difficult to wean. More than any other parrot, cockatoos seem to have serious emotional issues about being fed. It is more than nourishment for them—it is a matter of emotional security. This is true to a degree for all parrot chicks, but I've found other species more willing to grow up, whereas many cockatoos seem to relish the role of pam-

People with allergies can be especially sensitive to the feather dust and powdery nature of a cockatoo's plumage.

THE GUIDE TO OWNING A COCKATOO

pered baby. I've heard of two- and three-year-old cockatoos that still insist on being handfed, and will punish their owners by going on hunger strikes if forced to eat on their own. Although buying an unweaned parrot chick is almost always a bad idea, buying an unweaned cockatoo is always a very bad idea. Don't let anyone convince you otherwise.

HEALTH GUARANTEES

No matter where you decide to buy your cockatoo, you should always ask about the seller's health guarantee, and get it in writing if possible. Health guarantees vary widely—some give you just a day or two to visit a veterinarian and uncover any problems, whereas I've seen a few that will guarantee the baby's health for up to a year. Understand that almost all health guarantees offer to replace the bird or refund your money if a serious health problem arises, but I've never seen any that will agree to pay any vet bills incurred if you decide to keep and treat your new pet. If the unthinkable happens and your pet dies during the term of the health guarantee, refrigerate (do not freeze) the body and call the seller immediately. Most breeders and shops require that a qualified vet perform a necropsy (animal autopsy) to

A handfed cockatoo will be friendly and affectionate—and will probably enjoy a lot of petting and attention.

determine the cause of death before they honor the guarantee. After all, the bird could have died from an accident, or even sheer neglect, and its death was in no way the fault of the seller. At any rate, it's important that you read and fully understand the terms of the guarantee, so that if a health problem arises you know your rights and options.

If you've done your homework and purchased a healthy, friendly, fully weaned cockatoo chick from a reputable breeder or shop, you're in for a lifetime of love and companionship from your new pet. Now comes the best part: taking baby home.

Buying the Proper Cage

Before you bring your new pet home, you'll need to set up the cage. Parrot cages come in a wide variety of styles, materials, prices, and sizes, and choos-

Like other parrots, cockatoos enjoy sunlight and fresh air, so try to place your pet's cage near a window, but not in direct sunlight.

ing the right one might look like a daunting task for a new bird owner. Where do you begin?

CAGE PLACEMENT

Before you even consider buying a cockatoo, you must first decide where the cage will go. Cockatoos require relatively large cages, and you can't confine a bird to a too-small cage just because of space constraints in your home. If you don't have sufficient room, then don't get the bird. Ideally, the cage should be in a room where family members spend a great deal of time. Often, a family room or den is ideal. I don't recommend placing the cage in a bedroom, unless you want to be awakened at the crack of dawn each morning by an exuberant cockatoo ready to greet the new day. Kitchens aren't usually a good idea either, because cooking and cleaning fumes might pose a danger to your pet. And never place a parrot in a remote part of the house away from the family. Parrots are flock animals and want to be part of the action. A bird that's isolated will suffer from severe loneliness and will likely spend most of its time screaming for attention or plucking its feathers in frustration. Isolation is perhaps the cruelest punishment for a parrot. This is not to say you must spend every waking moment sitting at your bird's side. Cockatoos are extremely intelligent, and they will quickly learn that you must go to work or leave the house occasionally, but they will expect and demand some quality time with the family when you're at home. Again, don't buy a parrot unless you're willing to make the commitment.

CAGE SIZES AND MATERIALS

Once you've decided which species of cockatoo you're going to purchase, then you can look at cage sizing. Cockatoos vary widely in size, from the 12-inch Goffin's, to the huge Palm Cockatoos that can reach a length of 22 inches, so there is no "standard" size cockatoo cage. In general, small cockatoos such as Goffin's and Lesser Sulphur-crested require a cage size of at least 24 inches wide by 20 inches deep by 30 inches tall, with bar spacing between 5/8-inch and 1 inch. The medium to large cockatoos should be in a cage with minimum dimensions of

Cockatoos are active birds and will appreciate a cage design that allows them to climb around and exercise.

32 inches wide by 20 inches deep by 35 inches tall, with bar spacing between 7/8-inch and 1 inch. Please note that these are minimum recommended sizes; most cockatoos are active and playful, and they will appreciate the largest cage possible. Is it possible to get a cage that is too large? For cockatoos, probably not. Some species, especially many of the African parrots, seem to feel nervous and insecure in very large cages. In my experience, cockatoos like a lot of "turf," and they will spend their time

strutting around surveying their empire. If your bird shows any signs of feeling insecure in its large cage, you can add features such as open roosting boxes or sleeping huts (available in pet stores or many mail-order bird supply catalogs) to give it a place to feel safe when life gets too hectic.

When choosing a cockatoo cage, keep in mind that these are very strong, dexterous, and intelligent birds. A cockatoo will disassemble or destroy a flimsy, poorly made cage in short order. Mikey, my pet Moluccan, removed all the bolts and nuts holding

A travel cage like the Nylabone® Fold-Away Pet Carrier is an absolute necessity, even if you only use it for trips to the veterinarian.

Free time—in a safe and supervised location—is always an option in the home, but take care to protect furniture from droppings as well as strong claws and beaks.

his cage together one bored afternoon. Of course, the cage collapsed, much to his delight and my distress. He's now in a heavy welded wrought iron cage, which he hasn't been able to destroy, at least not yet. Your best bet for cockatoo containment is a cage made of heavy-duty plated wire, stainless steel, or powder-coated wrought iron. Never put a cockatoo in any cage with a wooden frame, unless you want to come home to a pile of sawdust and an escaped bird. Make sure the bars are reasonably thick and carefully welded: if you can flex the bars easily with your fingers, I guarantee your cockatoo will eventually work them loose. The cage should either be one-piece construction, or should have nuts and bolts that fit flush and are mostly out of the bird's easy reach. Don't think that you can simply tighten them enough so that the bird can't undo them. It might work for awhile, but cockatoos are amazingly persistent, and the larger species have incredible beak strength.

Because of that beak strength, it's important to buy a cage with a quality finish. Most wrought iron cages made today are powder-coated, which is a process that gives a very hard, baked-on type of finish. Some older cages, as well as some inexpensive imports, were simply painted metal that most parrots could chip with ease. Even powder-coated cages might eventually chip under the punishment of a cockatoo beak, but they hold their finish much better than cheaper models.

If you have the money to spend, stainless steel cages are the ultimate in parrot abodes. These won't rust, chip, discolor, or stain the way that wrought iron can, and their smooth non-reactive surface is very easy to clean. Unfortunately, they are very expensive—usually two or three times the price of a comparably sized wrought iron cage. They also can be somewhat difficult to find. Very few retail outlets sell them, so to purchase one you usually have to order straight from the manufacturer and have it shipped to you. You can find company listings on the Internet, or in magazines such as *Bird Talk*. Keep in mind that custom cages can take six to eight weeks to

Cockatoos are incredibly clever and persistent; sometimes a sturdy lock is the only way to keep one from escaping.

produce, so allow plenty of time before your bird is ready to come home.

Plated wire cages are another option, and these tend to be much less expensive than stainless or wrought iron. Unfortunately, there aren't very many of these available in sizes large enough for cockatoos. In general, silver-colored wire (usually nickel or zinc plate) holds up better than brass, which tends to wear off and discolor quickly. If you choose one of these

Playstands—which can be freestanding or mounted to the top of a cage—can be made of wood, natural branches, pipe, or PVC.

cages, make sure it is sturdy, of sufficient size, and all metal; those with plastic bases won't last long. Look carefully at the plating for chips, worn spots, or cracks. Run your fingers across the bars. If they feel rough or uneven, it might be a poorly plated cage that won't hold up well.

The Zinc Controversy

There have been some concerns raised lately about keeping birds in zinc-plated cages. Some veterinarians claim that birds ingest the zinc, which creates a myriad of problems, from feather picking to ill health. Cage manufacturers and many other vets dispute this, saying that the zinc used in the plating process is permanently bonded into the finish, and the birds can't possibly ingest any by chewing or biting the bars. Although zinc in trace amounts is a vital nutrient for both humans and birds, larger amounts are poisonous and can indeed lead to health problems. Although the jury is still out on this—both sides have compelling yet contradictory "proof"—I tend to believe that high quality zinc-plated cages are safe. Tests performed on birds in such cages have been inconsistent. Some birds show high levels of zinc in their systems, while others show completely normal ranges. On the other hand, some birds in zinc-free cages have high blood levels of the element. Because so many other factors, such as diet or genetic predisposition, can contribute to this problem, I think it's premature to assume that plated cages are dangerous, especially considering the long history of their use. If you have any concerns, you should discuss the issue with your avian veterinarian.

USED CAGES

Large parrot cages are pricey, so it can be very tempting to pick up a used cage through the classifieds. If you go this route, proceed with extreme caution. First of all, what happened to the previous occupant? If it held a bird that died from a contagious disease, you run a huge risk of exposing your new pet to the disease. Many avian viruses are extremely hardy and can survive a long time in the cracks and crevices of a cage, just waiting for their next victim. If you buy such a cage, you must thoroughly scrub and carefully disinfect every inch of it, which is not an easy task on a very large cage. Proper disinfection involves first scrubbing to remove all organic debris, then soaking the item for a minimum "contact time" (usually at least ten minutes) in the disinfectant, then careful rinsing. A parrot cage is obviously too large to immerse in a bucket of solution, so you'll have to continuously spray or wipe the cage with disinfectant, keeping it wet with the solution for the required contact time. A simple scrub and hose down with household cleaners will not do the job, and it will put

Many different types of toys are available for parrots, but be certain to choose those playthings that will stand up to a cockatoo's powerful beak.

your bird at serious risk.

Besides the danger of disease transmission, used cages come with a few other potential problems. Unless it's in pristine condition, you might just be buying a headache. If the finish is chipped or worn, it will be difficult to clean and might present a danger to your bird. If it has any broken or damaged pieces, you will not be able to get replacement parts unless you can identify the original manufacturer. Even then, the parts might be discontinued or unavailable, especially if it's an imported model. If parts are available, the price might make your "bargain buy" an expensive hassle. For

Perches of varying diameters and materials will allow your bird to flex his muscles and exercise his feet.

example, replacing the food crocks, perch, and bottom tray on a typical wrought iron cage could easily amount to 20 to 25 percent of the cost of a brand new cage. Choose your cockatoo's cage wisely, because you will both have to live with it for a very long time. A little extra money spent up front might be well worth the pleasure of having a sturdy, attractive, easy to clean, and functional home for your pet.

PERCHES

Once you choose a cage, your next step is outfitting it properly. Most new cages will come with a perch or two and food dishes, but you'll probably want to add to these basics. For healthy feet, parrots should have a variety of perch diameters and surfaces available. An adult parrot is on its feet 24 hours a day for life, and it never lies down unless it is sick or playing. Having just one perching surface is like a human having to wear the same pair of shoes every day of their life. The old-fashioned round dowel-type perches can be pretty uncomfortable for long-term use, causing pressure sores on a bird's feet because of their uniform diameter. If your cage comes with one of these, I would recommend replacing it with a natural branch perch. Because tree branches vary in shape and thickness along their length, they exercise the feet naturally. Manzanita and ribbonwood branches make great parrot perches, because their wood is smoothly textured, extremely hard and durable, and stands up well to large beaks. These are commonly included with large parrot cages, or you can purchase them separately from cage suppliers. Cholla cactus and grapevine are other choices, but both are softer than manzanita and much harder to clean due to their heavily textured surfaces.

Besides wood perches, there's a huge selection of other materials on the market today. Cement, sand, or terracotta "pedicure" perches are very popular now, and they claim to keep the bird's nails trimmed down. In my experience, they don't completely eliminate the need for periodic nail clipping, but they certainly help keep the sharp points dulled to a tolerable level. Some people express concern that these materials are too harsh and will cause foot irritation. I've found the opposite to be true: regular use of pedicure perches seems to toughen the feet slightly and keep them healthy and smooth. My birds really seem to like them, probably because they offer a sure-grip, non-slip texture.

Rope perches offer another option, but I don't recommend them as the main cage perch. They're soft on the feet, and their pliability makes them easy to hang from any spot in the cage, but they do have some inherent problems. First of all, they get dirty easily and are difficult to clean properly. You can't toss them in a washing machine, because their bolt end fasteners might damage or get jammed in the agitator. Running them through a dishwasher works pretty well, but you have to be careful to let them dry thoroughly or you run the risk of exposing your pet to molds and fungus. Secondly, they tend to fray and unwind. If your bird gets tangled in a frayed piece, it could be seriously injured or killed as it struggles to get free. I do use rope as a secondary perch in many of my cages, but when it starts to show wear, I toss it out and replace it.

Rope is a good option for perch materials, but it is difficult to clean and not recommended for use as the primary perch.

FOOD CUPS

Most new cages will include a set of food and water dishes, usually made of ceramic, plastic, or stainless steel. Though any of these will work, plastic tends to stain, and most cockatoos tend to chew plastic into tiny bits. Heavy-duty ABS plastic slows them

Some food cups can be fastened to playstands and perches; others are designed to be filled and replaced from outside a cage.

down, but they'll destroy it someday. I personally like stainless steel, because it's non-reactive, rust-resistant, and easy to clean and disinfect. The only problem with stainless steel is that it's very lightweight, which means that unless your cage has a holder that somehow locks down the cup, your cockatoo will most likely remove it from the holder and toss it (and its contents) across the cage. Cockatoos love to fling dishes and toss loose objects around. No one knows why, but the crock-flinging gene has been firmly implanted into all cockatoos in captivity.

If your cage isn't equipped with some kind of a lock-down device, your best bet is to go with a heavy ceramic crock. Sometimes the sheer weight of these will make it impossible for your bird to lift. Of course, some cockatoos are strong and ingenious enough to work even these loose from their hold-

THE GUIDE TO OWNING A COCKATOO

ers, or else they chip away at the ceramic with their beaks, scattering sharp little shards about. If your bird does this, there are some clever locking crocks available that attach to the cage and require a high degree of dexterity and an opposable thumb to remove them. Of course, they're never as easy and convenient to remove and replace as those that simply drop into the cage holder, so I use them only as my last line of defense.

When you finally decide on what type of dish to use, go out and buy a duplicate or triplicate set. With just one set of dishes, it's easy to get careless about hygiene. In your morning rush, it'll be tempting to dump new food on top of the old, or to give the water dish a cursory swipe with the sponge before refilling it. With two sets, I fill the clean dishes, pull the dirty ones from the cage, and toss them directly into the dishwasher. The next morning, there's a fresh clean set waiting for me. If you don't run your dishwasher on a daily basis, then get two or three extra sets so that there are always clean ones available. Of course, if you don't have a dishwasher, you'll have to clean them carefully by hand, but having a few sets still makes life easier on those days you're rushed for time.

CAGE LITTERS AND LINERS

There are many different types of cage litters available, including pine shavings, corncob, ground walnut shells, and pelleted grass fibers. I don't recommend any of them. Although they give the cage a nice appearance, they contribute greatly to the time and expense of cage upkeep. If they're not changed every few days, they can har-

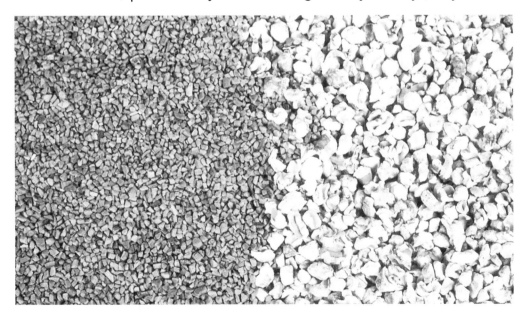

Although ground-up walnut shells and corncob can be used as cage litter, they can be expensive and prone to high levels of bacteria buildup.

As with any perch material, it's a good idea to regularly clean natural branches of droppings and other debris.

bor dangerous levels of mold and bacteria. It doesn't look too bad, and it's a pain in the neck to change it, so it's easy to scoop out the obvious crud and leave the rest. This is a really dangerous practice that can endanger your bird.

Even if you're willing to invest the time, money, and labor necessary to put fresh litter down several times a week, your cockatoo will most likely scatter the stuff everywhere and make a terrible mess. I did this for a few years, replacing vacuum cleaners more often than most people change their socks. Now I only use paper on the cage bottoms. Newspaper works just fine, although some cockatoos will tear it up and rub the ink all over their bodies, turning themselves a very unpleasant shade of gray. Newspaper ink is non-toxic, but definitely unflattering on white feathers. I buy a special white, lightly waxed paper that is custom cut to fit my cage bottoms. Each day, I simply roll up the old paper, toss it in the garbage, and put a fresh piece down. It takes just seconds, and the cage floor is always clean and neat. If you don't want to use newspaper or spend the money for custom liners like I do, you can buy large rolls of brown Kraft paper from packaging stores or suppliers. Freezer paper (the heavy white waxed stuff used by old-fashioned butchers) works great too. Don't use colored gift-wrap papers, because some of these might contain lead or other dangerous chemicals. Of course, not too many people would gift-wrap their cage floors, but don't let your bird ever chew or play with the stuff either.

Parrots love to chew, so you might find that your bird immediately rushes to the floor and gleefully rips the paper to shreds. If this happens, you have a few options. If your cage will allow, move the grate up a few inches so that the bird can no longer reach the bottom tray. Because a determined cockatoo has a very long reach, this might not work. You can replace the paper as fast as the bird tears it up, in the hopes that it will eventually tire of the game and quit, but I've found that most owners tire much faster than their birds. I've resigned myself to sweeping up bits of torn paper from around the cages of my paper shredders. It's still a lot cheaper, and it's easier on the vacuum than corncob.

TRAVEL CAGES

Now that you have the main cage set up, it's time to think about a travel cage. Even if you never plan to take your bird anywhere, travel cages are vital for emergencies or trips to the vet or groomer. If you plan on taking your cockatoo with you on trips, you'll need a small but sturdy cage that folds down or is easy to disassemble. Some manufacturers sell collapsible dog crates that fold up to the size of a suitcase, complete with carrying handle. Add a perch and many of these will work great for medium to large parrots. Make sure whatever you get is sturdy enough that your bird can't destroy it before your trip is over.

If you aren't planning any long jaunts, but just need something to get your pet back and forth from the vet's office, you can use one of the heavy plastic "pet taxis" sold for dogs and cats. These come in many sizes and usually have a metal grate front door, which your bird can hold onto during the trip. If you're handy with a drill, it's easy to further customize these for parrot use. Simply cut a perch to fit tightly from one side of the carrier to the other. Drill a small hole through the plastic on each side, then into both ends of the perch. Fasten screws through the plastic and into the perch ends, and you now have a parrot taxi. Keep in mind that these are intended just for short trips, and should not be used to house a bird overnight. Most parrots will get fed up with such restrictive quarters and will chew their way through the plastic to freedom. These carriers usually are airline approved, so they also can be used for shipping live birds. Even if you can't imagine needing a carrier, you'll be very happy to have one on hand if an emergency arises.

Feeding Your Cockatoo

If you want to insure a long and healthy life for your cockatoo, the first place to begin is with proper nutrition. A poor

A varied diet—complete with pellets, seeds, and fresh fruits and vegetables—is the best way to ensure your bird's good health.

diet will shorten your pet's life span dramatically, not only from the direct effect of malnutrition, but also by weakening the bird's immune system and making it much more susceptible to disease. I've heard it said repeatedly by avian veterinarians: the vast majority of illnesses encountered in pet birds are caused or exacerbated by improper diet.

SEED MIXES

It's often tempting to grab a bag of one of the many fortified seed mixes touted as a basic diet. Since the early 1950s, seed mixes have gained a wide market and a reputation as an appropriate diet for parrots. There are several selling points for seed. It's cheap, can be stored for several months (often even a few years) without showing obvious signs of spoilage, and parrots love it. Unfortunately, although it's

30

It's no fun to eat the same thing day after day; new foods and treats will add some excitement to your bird's life.

fine for an occasional snack, it makes a lousy diet. It would be the equivalent of a human trying to survive on a diet of nothing but potato chips and grilled cheese sandwiches. It might be fun for awhile, but your health would suffer greatly.

Seed is extremely high in fat and deficient in calcium, vitamins A, D_3, K, B_{12}, C, many other trace elements, and some amino acids. Although all parrots do poorly on a seed-only diet, cockatoos are especially prone to developing illnesses, including fatty tumors, liver and kidney disease, and cardiovascular problems. Supple-menting with vitamins and minerals might correct some of the nutrient deficiencies,

but it will do nothing to prevent long-term damage from such a high-fat diet. There are people (especially on the Internet) who will tell you that seed is fine, and they've been feeding it to their pet bird for many years. The problem with their argument is that the damage from malnutrition is slow and subtle, until death is imminent. Perhaps their bird has had a sinus infection or two (most likely caused by vitamin A deficiency). Maybe its feathers are oily-looking or its beak is overgrown (possible signs of liver damage). Or maybe it always looked healthy, until it died at age 15 from "old age." (Cockatoos have a potential life span of 50 to 70 years or more; a 15-year-old cockatoo is most definitely not old.)

FORMULATED DIETS

So what then should you feed your bird? Although much research still is being done on avian nutrition, most experts agree that a base diet of 70 to

Parrot food mixes can be purchased or created at home, using a combination of nuts, pellets, seeds, and dried veggies and fruits.

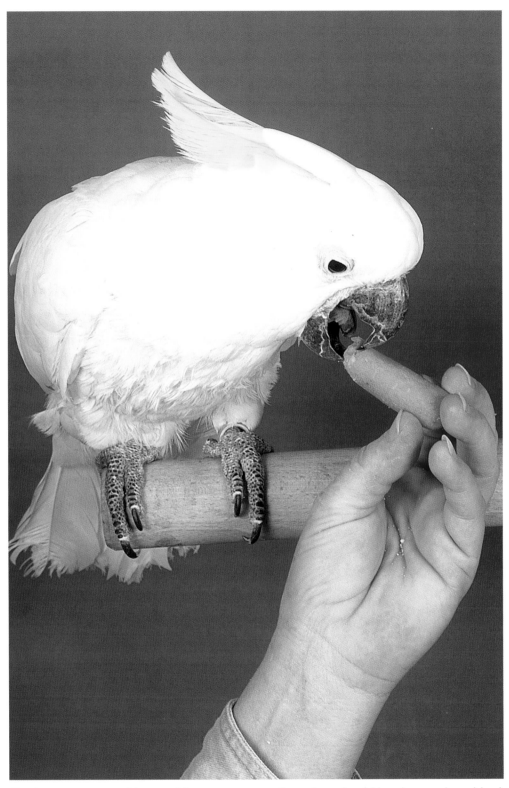

Fresh carrots are nutritious and fun to gnaw on; all produce should be clean and scrubbed free of pesticides or other chemicals.

THE GUIDE TO OWNING A COCKATOO

80 percent formulated parrot food, with a wide array of fruits, vegetables, grains, seeds, beans, and nuts comprising the other 20 to 30 percent, will keep your pet in prime health. Formulated parrot diets come in two forms—pelleted and extruded— although most people in the avian community use the term "pellets" to refer to both types. In general, true pellets consist of a mixture of coarsely ground grains and other food products, supplemented with vitamins and minerals, and pressed into hard, cylindrical pieces. These diets tend to be tan or light brown in color and have a natural grain aroma. Extruded diets begin with much the same ingredients, which are then finely ground, cooked to enhance digestibility, and forced through a die and shaped in a process called extrusion. Extruded brands often contain flavorings and colorings and are available in a wide variety of shapes, colors, and sizes. The bottom line is that either of these formulations will make a wonderful and healthy base for your bird's diet. To choose a brand, ask either your avian veterinarian or breeder for a recommendation, or experiment with several until you find one or more that appeal to your pet. I've found four or five manufacturers that I trust and that my birds like, so I switch between them frequently to prevent boredom in my flock. Parrots don't seem to suffer digestive upsets like dogs can when their brand of food

is changed abruptly, and this method prevents the food fixations that cockatoos are prone to developing when they eat the same thing every day.

FRUITS, VEGGIES, AND PEOPLE FOOD

Although formulated foods are marketed as complete diets, and birds can live on these alone, I think it's necessary for your parrot's mental well-being to offer it plenty of fresh foods. No matter how healthy, a diet composed solely of dry pellets might get pretty boring. Juicy sweet fresh fruits, colorful vegetables, and fresh nuts and grains offer variety and extra nutrition. Just make sure that these items don't exceed about 30 percent of what your pet eats in a day, or you run the risk of unbalancing the diet. I usually give my birds a small piece of fruit and a few nuts in the morning, along with fresh pellets in their bowl at all times. At night, they get a small serving of fruits, veggies, or "people food."

Parrots have nutritional needs very

A pelleted diet is largely comprised of ground grains; it can be supplemented with a variety of fresh foods.

similar to humans, so almost anything that's good for you probably will be good for your cockatoo. Most birds adore pizza and pasta, cooked meats, and cheese. Whole grain pastas and breads provide a healthy and filling snack. Don't give your pet avocados, chocolate, alcohol, or caffeine, which are each toxic to birds, and always use common sense when it comes to high-fat or salt-laden foods. My birds love an occasional french fry, but this is a rare treat. And be careful with dairy products. Although these are a good source of calcium and usually a coveted treat, parrots lack the enzyme to properly digest milk products, so large

There's a treat for every taste out there, but it may take some experimentation to find the right delicacy for your cockatoo.

quantities might upset their digestive tracts. Small portions of cottage cheese, hard cheeses, and yogurt are fine and won't cause your pet any trouble.

When feeding fruits and vegetables, aim for nutrient-dense choices. Although most birds love apples, grapes, and corn, these aren't packed with nearly as many vitamins as, say, sweet potatoes or kale. Most cockatoos tend to go crazy for fresh corn on the cob, and they will wolf down every last kernel, but you should try to sneak in some broccoli and carrots, too. Always scrub fruits and veggies carefully to remove dirt and pesticide residue. Most grocery stores now carry cleaning sprays made especially for washing produce. These usually contain citrus oils, which safely break down many contaminants and rinse them away. Scrubbing won't always remove all pesticides, but it will reduce the levels considerably. Never allow your bird (or anyone else in your family, for that matter) to eat unwashed produce, even if it's labeled "organic." Organic fruits and veggies are grown without chemical pesticides, but might still harbor invisible molds, bacteria, or chemical over-spray from neighboring farms. Always wash carefully. And always remove any uneaten soft foods from the cage after a few hours, because bacteria can multiply rapidly and endanger your pet.

SEEDS, GRAINS, AND NUTS

Seeds, nuts, and whole grains—in addition to fruits and veggies—can help round out a healthy parrot diet. As discussed before, seed should be fed very sparingly, but a tablespoon or so a few times a week will be a welcome treat. Always buy the freshest seed available in small quantities, and keep it in the freezer if possible. Seed goes rancid pretty quickly when stored in hot humid conditions, and it can grow molds and fungi that produce dangerous compounds called mycotoxins. There are many different types of mycotoxins, but they're all potentially deadly. Aflatoxin is a common type found on peanuts and corn; it is a highly potent carcinogen that usually attacks the liver.

Though crops intended for human consumption are tested for contamination, molds can attack and produce these toxins at any time with improper storage, so even "safe" crops might go bad later if mishandled. Although the toxins themselves are invisible, the presence of molds or fungi always indicates that the food is unfit for consumption and should be discarded. Never feed any seed, nut, or grain that looks moldy, shriveled, or otherwise odd, or that smells musty or rancid. Don't buy seed from a store's bulk bins, which greatly increase the danger of all sorts of contamination. Some seed mix manufacturers are now offering poly-bagged seed that has been

Millet spray is a favorite treat of most birds that is best reserved for special occasions.

flushed with carbon dioxide before sealing. This process forces oxygen out of the bag, which kills any bugs that might have been on the seed, reduces oxidation, and helps to preserve nutrients. Although there's no guarantee that the seed was fresh to begin with, these brands are likely to remain fresh on the shelf longer than those packed in regular bags.

When buying whole nuts, I suggest that you stick with human-grade varieties from the supermarket. Although animal-grade peanuts are also supposed to be checked for aflatoxin levels, I'm less comfortable with how they're handled, processed, and stored after inspection. I've spoken to a few well-known bird-treat manufacturers

Special parrot-rearing formulas can be handfed to unweaned baby cockatoos, either with a bent spoon or with a syringe.

about this issue, and I was surprised and happy to hear that many of them use only human-grade peanuts in their treats because they share the same concerns. Buy only raw or roasted unsalted peanuts, and limit your bird to just a few a week. Walnuts, almonds, pecans, pine nuts, unsalted pistachios, Brazil nuts, and filberts can provide a nutritious treat, although you might need to crack the larger nuts for your pet. Most cockatoos can handle walnuts (a great source of vitamin E), and almonds (high in calcium), but Brazil nuts and filberts are usually too difficult for all but the very largest species.

OTHER FOODS

Before the advent of formulated parrot diets, many breeders recognized the need for a reliable source of nutrition for their birds, and they began experimenting with foods designed for other animals. Dry dog food, zoo primate diets (monkey chow), and commercial turkey pellets all found their way into parrot dishes. Most of these products don't work well for pet birds. Dog food, which contains animal byproducts, can also contain unaccept-ably high levels of gram-negative bacteria. Although this won't bother your dog, it might sicken a bird, especially one already stressed from other factors. Turkey pellets aren't a good idea, either. These are designed to fatten a bird for Thanksgiving dinner, with little concern for long-term effects. Few turkeys make it much past their first birthday, so it should be obvious that their diet is going to be quite different from that of a cockatoo, which might have a life span comparable to humans.

Dry primate diets still remain popular among some breeders of large cockatoos and macaws. These biscuits are fine for an occasional treat, but I don't recommend feeding them on a daily basis. They too can contain gram-negative bacteria, although probably not at the levels found in dog food. They're also very high in protein, which can be tough on a bird's kidneys. Cockatoos tend to tolerate high protein levels better than some other parrots, but I'd still feed this in limited amounts. Some manufacturers, concerned that people were turning away from feeding their birds monkey biscuits, simply repackage the stuff and label it "parrot biscuits." Same product, different packaging—your best defense is to be an educated consumer.

SUPPLEMENTS

If your pet is eating a healthy diet like the one described above, then you don't need to add any additional vitamins or minerals, unless recommended by your veterinarian. If your bird is a finicky eater and hasn't yet made the transition to a healthy diet, then some supplementation might be in order. Keep in mind that too high a dosage of vitamins is just as dangerous as a defi-ciency, so don't fall into the "more-is-better" mind trap. Always follow the manufacturer's recommendations, and don't double up on products. For example, if you're using a general-purpose multivitamin, check the label to see if it also contains minerals such as calcium. If it does, it's probably not necessary to add other sources, like mineral blocks or calcium powders. You'll find that there's a wide array of nutritional supplements on the market, all promising to make your bird healthy, beautiful, and happy. Many of these are excellent products and can act as insurance for birds on a marginal diet, but nothing can truly make up for the long-term effects of poor food choices.

Although your cockatoo might like to be involved in its food preparation, the kitchen is not the safest place for a bird.

Gently remove formula or food from a bird's face and beak before it dries and hardens.

Besides vitamins and minerals, there are a few other products out there that bear mentioning. Probiotics are beneficial bacteria that colonize the digestive tract and crowd out some unwelcome pathogens. They also play a part in the digestive process. You're probably familiar with yogurt's *lactobacillus* bacteria, which is an active probiotic. Some pellets already contain probiotics, but there apparently is no danger of oversupplementing with these; the excess simply passes through the bird's system. Although these additives aren't strictly necessary for healthy birds, there's certainly no harm in using them. If your bird is ever sick, especially if it is being treated with antibiotics, then probiotics are vital to help restore the digestive flora and fight off secondary yeast infections. I sprinkle a probiotic powder on soft food for all my birds once every week or so. During breeding season, when they're more stressed, I use it a few times a week. If I have a sick bird, I use it at every feeding for that bird.

Digestive enzymes are another potentially beneficial supplement. These enzymes are usually sold in a powdered form that can be sprinkled on soft food. They help break down the food and are thought to make the nutrients easier to assimilate. Again, some pellets already contain them. Few studies have been done to show how helpful they might be for healthy birds, but they appear to be quite safe at recommended dosages, and they might be worth a try. Ask your veterinarian for an opinion.

Unfortunately, there are a few supplements on the market that can be harmful. There's a persistent notion in the pet community that birds need grit to digest their food. Although this is true for some birds, such as canaries and pigeons, parrots do *not* need grit. In fact, if they swallow too much it can impact in their gizzard, causing severe illness or death. Most cockatoos have enough sense to avoid eating ground rock, but it's best if you don't offer it to them in the first place. Another troublesome item is charcoal. Touted as a "blood purifier," this stuff moves through the digestive tract absorbing all kinds of things, including valuable nutrients. Although veterinarians use activated charcoal short-term in a few limited situations to pull toxins from the body, you should never feed this to your pet without veterinary supervision. It has absolutely no benefit for healthy birds, and repeated use will cause severe depletion of necessary nutrients.

WATER

No chapter on nutrition is complete without a brief discussion of the importance of clean, fresh water. Most people don't think of water as a nutrient, but it is perhaps the most important nutrient of all. All of your bird's bodily functions depend on water, and a loss of only 10 percent of the body's water means death. Always keep your pet's water dish clean and full. Most parrots love to make "soup" by tossing toys, food, and poop into their water dish. This mess grows bacteria amazingly fast and quickly becomes a health hazard. Always change the water at least once a day. For determined soup-makers, you might have to change it two or three times daily. If this seems like too much of a hassle, there are parrot water bottles on the market that hang from the side of the cage and dispense water when the bird presses its tongue against the valve end. Although these work great for many parrots, in my experience cockatoos either take them apart, jam food into the valve to stop it up, or hold the valve open while the water all drains out onto the floor. It makes a great toy for a bored cockatoo but won't solve the water problem. If you do go this route, you still need to change the water and wash the bottle daily, and check it frequently to make sure that the water is flowing properly.

If possible, check the quality of your water. This is important for your family's health as well as that of your bird.

Walnuts, almonds, and other nuts are nutritious—although somewhat fatty—treats; part of the fun is in cracking the shell to get to the nut.

Breeding cockatoos have special nutritional needs; consult a breeder or avian vet for advice.

Municipal water supplies are tested regularly and the reports should be available to all users. If you have a private well, or suspect that you might have contamination problems such as lead in your home plumbing, you can have your water tested for a reasonable fee. Contact your county offices for referral to a reputable lab. Unless your tap water is really nasty, it should be safe for your bird. If you do find that you have water problems, you might want to consider one of the many water purification systems available for home use, or switch to bottled water for drinking and cooking.

I've found that, in my quest to provide the best possible care for my birds, I'm often making lifestyle changes that I'd never thought about before, but that end up being beneficial for me and my family. May your new cockatoo be a catalyst for healthy changes in your life.

Cockatoo Health Care

With a nutritious diet, proper caging, and lots of love, your cockatoo is well on the road to a long healthy life. Now is the time to think about preventative and emergency health care.

Accidents and illness can strike without warning, but a little advance planning on your part might mean the difference between life and death for your bird.

Choose an avian veterinarian ahead of time, even before you bring your new cockatoo home.

CHOOSING A VETERINARIAN

Your first and most important step is to find a qualified avian veterinarian. Do not wait until you "need" a vet to begin looking. By then it might be too late to save your pet. Parrots are masters at hiding illness. In the wild, a noticeably sick or weak bird would be the first one targeted by a hungry predator in search of an easy lunch. Because of this deeply bred instinct for survival, a sick parrot will use every last bit of its strength to "keep up with the flock," and to convince the world that it feels just fine. By the time your bird is showing obvious signs of illness, it is already very, very sick, and too weak to keep up the charade. Trust me; you don't want to be flipping through the phone book, trying to track down an

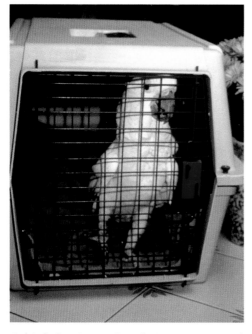

A bird that is used to being in its travel carrier will be less stressed by a trip to the veterinarian, especially if it is ill.

animal hospital that will see birds while your beloved pet is on the cage floor bleeding or gasping for breath.

The best time to choose a vet is before you even bring your new bird home. Most health guarantees require a veterinary exam within a few days of purchase anyhow, so you're better off doing your homework in advance. If possible, schedule the exam the same day you're picking up your pet, and go straight from the seller to the animal hospital. This way, you'll know immediately if there are any problems that need addressing, and you won't have to stress the bird by taking it out again just a few days after it begins to settle into its new home. Don't assume that you can simply bring your cockatoo to the same veterinarian who cares for your other pets. Avian medicine is highly specialized, and even the most remarkably qualified dog and cat vets might be totally lost when it comes to caring for birds. An honest practitioner will tell you this up front, but there are some who might try to muddle through with their limited experience, and your bird will suffer as a result.

If you're lucky enough to live near an avian specialist, then look no further. You can identify these board-certified veterinarians by the initials ABVP after their names. This means that they have passed rigorous testing by the American Board of Veterinary Practitioners in their area of specialty. If you find a practitioner with ABVP,

Avian Practice, after his/her name, you'll know you've found a highly qualified bird specialist. In reality, however, these folks are few and far between, so unless you live in a big city or near a veterinary college, you're not likely to find one.

Your next best choice is any veterinarian who treats birds on a regular basis, and who is a member of the Association of Avian Veterinarians (AAV). This professional group keeps its members abreast of the latest developments in avian medicine and provides fellowship and support. I believe that AAV membership is an excellent indicator of a veterinarian's interest in and level of knowledge about avian clients. You can find an AAV member in your area by calling the association at 561-393-8901 or by using their web site at www.aav.org.

Of course, there are many excellent veterinarians out there who don't belong to professional organizations for one reason or another. Ask your local pet shop or breeder for recommendations or contact a bird club in your area. Often, other bird people can give you the best evaluation of a local practitioner or clinic. Don't be afraid to "interview" a vet by phone before you decide to make an appointment, but use common sense. Keep your questions short and to the point, be courteous, and schedule the call for a convenient time. Don't expect a polite response if you catch the doctor

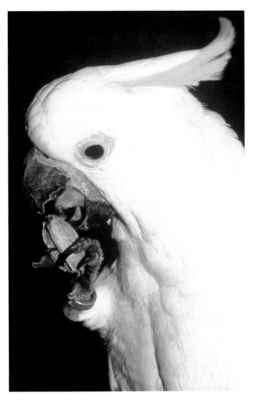

Nuts and other foods can be contaminated with bacteria or fungi, so only buy from stores that sell clean and fresh products.

between emergencies and demand that he or she waste a valuable chunk of time answering a long rambling list of questions that you bark out like a drill sergeant. Some pertinent questions are, How many birds do you see in a week? Who handles your clients when you're out of town? Are you on call for after-hours emergencies? If not, where do you refer emergencies? These are all important points to consider before you make your choice.

THE NEW BIRD EXAM

Once you've found a veterinarian you like, schedule an appointment as close as possible to when you're picking up your pet. Don't be surprised if the first part of your visit focuses on you and how you plan on caring for your bird. A good vet knows that an educated owner is one of the best assurances that a parrot will remain healthy. The doctor also might use this time to casually observe the bird while it's sitting in its carrier, to detect things like labored breathing, lameness, or abnormal behaviors. My talented and funny vet has a term she uses for these subtle signs of illness: "ADR" (ain't doin' right).

During the hands-on portion of the exam, the doctor will weigh your bird

Cheek-puffing is usually a sign of contentment, but it can also mean that your bird is cold, sleepy, or not well.

and look at its eyes, ears, nose, mouth, and vent for signs of swelling, discharge, inflammation, or infection. Weight loss is often the first sign of illness in birds, so it's important to make sure your cockatoo is within normal weight range for its species. Once you know your pet's healthy weight, this will be a valuable indicator during future exams. The vet will listen to the bird's heart and respiratory system with a stethoscope to make sure everything sounds normal, and gently tug on or bend the wings and legs to check for signs of lameness or discomfort.

Once the physical exam is over, there are several diagnostic tests that the doctor might recommend. A CBC, or complete blood count, is a very common test that uses a small amount of blood, usually drawn from a clipped toenail. This test gives a wealth of information about the bird's health by examining the different components of its blood. Another more detailed blood test, often called a serum chemistry, or chemistry panel, offers even more information, and can detect many problems at a very early stage.

Besides blood work, there are other tests that use body fluids to detect suspected bacterial or fungal diseases. Using a sterile cotton swab, the vet will gather a fluid sample, usually from the bird's cloaca. (The cloaca, or vent, is the common opening on a bird's posterior end from which it passes urine, feces, and sperm or

It's a good idea to monitor your birds' weight to gauge its health; weight loss is a sure sign that something may be wrong with your pet.

eggs). For a gram stain, this sample is then smeared on a microscopic slide and treated with special dyes. This test allows the doctor to get an idea of the type and quantity of bacteria in the bird's system. If the bacterial count is too high, or of the wrong type, the vet might suggest a culture and sensitivity test. In this test, the sample fluid is streaked across a laboratory culture plate and placed in an incubator to encourage the pathogens to grow. After 24 to 48 hours, the lab can identify the species of bacteria, gauge the growth, and determine which antibiotics stand the best chance of fighting it.

COMMON DISEASES

Your veterinarian also might recommend testing for certain specific diseases. Psittacosis, (also known as Ornithosis, Chlamydiosis, and "parrot fever") is a relatively common disease in some pet birds, although improved testing and treatment have reduced its occurrence considerably, especially in large parrots. It's still common in small birds like budgies, lovebirds, and cockatiels. Psittacosis can be transmitted to humans, where it causes a flu-like illness. It's very unlikely that a healthy adult would contract a disease from a pet parrot, but households with elderly or immune-suppressed individuals

Exercise and healthy foods are especially important for Rose-breasted cockatoos, which are prone to obesity and tumors.

should always exercise great caution and have all birds tested.

Although less common than psittacosis, there are a few very deadly viruses that can infect parrots. None of these are transmissible to humans, but if you already have pet birds be cautious about bringing new birds into the house until they get a clean bill of health, or you will be putting your existing pets at risk. The four most common (and most deadly) viruses are Psittacine Beak and Feather Disease (PBFD), Proventricular Dilatation Disease (PDD), Pacheco's virus, and Polyomavirus. Of these diseases, PBFD and PDD are always fatal, and only a very few birds survive active infections of Pacheco's or Polyoma. There are screening tests available for PBFD, Polyoma, and Pacheco's, but not for PDD. Some of these tests will only indicate if a bird has been exposed to the disease, however, and don't always indicate clinical disease. Vaccines exist for Polyoma and Pacheco's, but there is some disagreement in the veterinary community about their safety and efficacy. Your best bet is to buy a healthy baby from a reliable source and then listen to your veterinarian's advice regarding testing and disease screening.

ACCIDENTS AND FIRST AID

In reality, it's unlikely you'll encounter any of these diseases unless you purchase an already-sick baby, or expose your pet to other sick birds at bird fairs or shows. For most pets, the biggest health danger comes from poor nutrition and accidents. If you follow the advice given in the nutrition chapter, then you won't have to worry about nutritionally related problems. Accidents, unfortunately, can happen despite your best care. Fortunately, there are a few precautions you can take that will greatly increase your pet's chances of survival.

First of all, clipping your bird's wings can prevent many accidents. I mention wing-clipping in several places throughout this book, but I can't emphasize it enough: an unclipped bird is an accident waiting to happen. I've spoken with countless people who have told me "My bird would never fly away," or "He's too smart to fly into a wall," or "She never flies…I don't think she knows how to fly." Invariably, they're the same people who call me for grief counseling when their beloved pet gets spooked and flies away forever, or slams into a mirror and breaks its neck. Keep your cockatoo's wings clipped. Secondly, supervise your bird at all times when it's out of its cage. It only takes a second for an unwatched parrot to bite into an electrical cord, get attacked by another pet, or get tangled in something. If you must leave the room, put your pet back in its cage where it will be safe.

If an accident occurs despite all your precautions, your bird's life will depend on how well you respond. I recommend keeping a small first aid kit handy, stocked with sterile gauze, styptic powder (to stop minor bleeding), tweezers, a heating pad, an iodine compound (Betadine™ is one nationally known brand), and clorhexadine solution (available mail-order or from your veterinarian.) You should also keep emergency phone numbers for your vet and a poison-control hotline handy. In most cases, your best bet will

Clipping your cockatoo's wings will prevent him from flying into trouble. The feathers will grow in gradually.

Spray baths and misting are much enjoyed by most cockatoos; regular misting and preening will help maintain healthy plumage.

be to get your pet to the animal clinic as quickly as possible. In the meantime, there are a few steps you can take to help your bird survive.

First, determine the cause of the accident. Is the bird unconscious? Bleeding? Burned? Drowning? Are any broken bones evident? If the bird is unconscious or appears in shock, place a heating pad in a small box and cover it with a soft clean towel. Place the bird gently on the towel and get it to a vet as fast as possible. Make sure there's adequate air circulation and watch the bird carefully for signs of overheating. Sick and injured birds lose body heat very quickly, and simply keeping them warm can be a critical tactic in keeping them alive. Most sporting goods stores sell small disposable, non-toxic air-activated heating pads that are used as

hand-warmers by sportsmen. They're inexpensive (a few dollars each) and make wonderful emergency heaters for birds and reptiles. I always keep some in my house and car.

If the bird is bleeding, you need to act very quickly. First, determine the source of the blood. Often, parrots will break emerging feathers that are still encased in a protective sheath. These are called "blood feathers," and they can bleed heavily. If there is just a tiny bit of blood (one or two drops), you can put the bird in a quiet place for a few minutes and see if the bleeding stops on its own. In some cases, these will coagulate and stop bleeding, but you'll have to keep an eye out for re-injury to the area. If it's only minor damage, the feather will continue to grow, but if it's badly broken, it will usually die off and molt out within a few weeks. If the bleeding doesn't stop after a few minutes, then you will have to pull out the broken feather. With a large cockatoo, this will be a two-person job. Wrap the bird gently in a towel to restrain it. While one person holds the bird, the other person should extend the wing and grasp it firmly at a point directly above the broken feather. With a pair of needle-nose pliers, grip the broken feather near where it emerges from the skin and pull it quickly in the direction it grows. This does hurt, and your bird will not be very happy, but it must be done or your pet might bleed to death. If

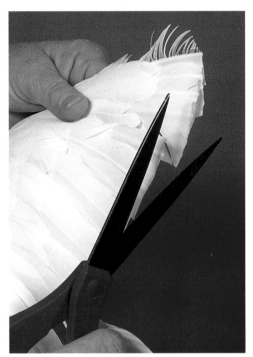

A cockatoo with clipped wings is less likely to be injured in household accidents. Always point the scissors away from a bird's body.

A five-week-old Umbrella cockatoo still requires consistent and frequent hand-feeding.

there is any bleeding at the feather follicle, hold gentle pressure against the spot with sterile gauze until the bleeding stops. It's very important that you immobilize the wing directly above the damaged feather, or you risk breaking the wing when you pull on the feather. If possible, ask your veterinarian to demonstrate this procedure and proper methods of restraint during your bird's first exam.

If your bird is bleeding from its nose or mouth, or from a large skin wound, keep it warm and get it to the vet immediately. In the case of a skin wound, hold gentle pressure against the area with sterile gauze to slow the bleeding. Even if the bleeding stops,

Careful thought and proper planning can prevent most accidental injuries. Even choosing safe and appropriate toys can make a difference.

cockatoo will likely die. Even a tiny, barely noticeable scratch can put the bacteria into your bird's system and cause death. A simple course of antibiotics can prevent this tragedy, so please don't ignore the danger.

If your pet is burned, don't ever use human burn ointment. These are greasy and can foul the feathers and interfere with their insulating properties, causing the bird to become chilled. They're also not intended for ingestion, and if your pet attempts to preen its feathers and swallows the ointment, it might be poisoned. If the burn is small and superficial (for example, the bird steps onto a burning cigarette) run cool (not cold) water over the spot for a minute or two, and call your vet for advice. If the burn is serious or the bird appears to be in shock, keep it warm and get to an emergency clinic immediately.

you must still seek emergency care immediately. Your pet might require antibiotics, sutures, or replacement fluids. If it is a very small wound with minor blood loss, and the bird seems alert and active, you can cleanse the area with clorhexadine solution, rinse carefully, and apply an iodine solution. Watch carefully for signs of infection or irritation, and call your veterinarian for further instructions. The one thing you must *never* ignore is a cat bite or scratch. Cats carry a bacterium in their saliva that is absolutely deadly to birds, and without proper antibiotics your

As you've probably realized by now, most accidents and illnesses require veterinary assistance. Although common sense first aid is important in emergencies, never try to "doctor" your pet at home with over-the-counter medications. Most of these are useless, and many can be downright dangerous. I've spoken to far too many grief-stricken owners who lost their beloved pet because they tried to save a few bucks by avoiding a vet visit. A qualified avian veterinarian is your best resource, and your bird's best hope for a long and healthy life.

The Well-Behaved Cockatoo

A well-behaved pet cockatoo is perhaps one of the most pleasurable companions you'll ever find. The key words, however, are "well-behaved." An untrained, undisciplined parrot can be a nightmare, a spoiled beast that tries your sanity at every turn. You need to understand, however, that your bird's behavior depends mostly on you. If you want a well-trained pet, it's up to you to set guidelines and carry them out with loving discipline.

THE BASICS

The first step in parrot training is to make sure that the bird's wings are properly clipped. It is impossible to train an unclipped bird; it will simply fly away rather than obey. Your local veterinarian, bird breeder, or bird shop probably does wing clips, and they can show you how to perform

this essential grooming procedure at home if you prefer. Once your pet is clipped, you can begin with training of

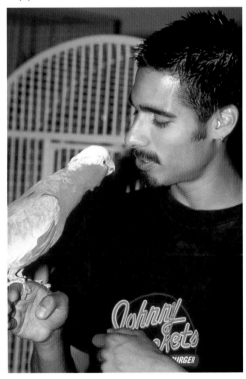

Living with and caring for a cockatoo will be more pleasurable if your pet is hand-tamed and somewhat behaved.

Once a bird's wings are clipped, you can concentrate on training without as much worry about escape and injury.

two basic commands: "step up" and "get down."

"Step up" is the command you will use to pick up your cockatoo and move it from place to place. Start by placing the bird on a training stand or on the back of a sturdy wooden or metal chair. Place your wrist against the bird's body right above its legs and say "step up" while pushing firmly but gently against it. (Please note that training manuals geared toward small birds will say to press your finger against the bird; most cockatoos are way too big to perch on a human finger, so you need to offer your wrist, forearm, or the side of your hand.) If your pet climbs up onto your arm, praise it lavishly. If it leans back, bites, or otherwise tries to escape the command, say "No!" in a firm voice and try again. The key is to push against the bird in a fluid motion to slightly disturb its balance so that it steps up. You certainly don't want to push so hard that you knock it off the perch, but if you hold your arm passively against the bird it will most likely not understand what you want it to do. If your pet continues to resist, place your other hand on its back and push forward slightly at the same time you're offering your wrist. Most tame birds learn this command very quickly, but be consistent. Never allow your bird to turn and walk away from you after you've given the "step up" command, or you will simply teach it that obedience is optional.

Once you have your pet climbing onto your arm with ease, the next command to teach is "get down." This is simply the reverse of "step up," and it is the command you'll use to place your bird on a playstand or back in its cage. While your bird is on your arm, place it in front of the training perch or chair back and say "get down." Make sure that you've placed the bird close enough and at a suitable height so that it can step off easily. As you give the command, tilt your arm *slightly* so

Two cockatoos may keep each other company, but it's likely that they will become more bonded to each other than to you.

that the bird leans forward and reaches for the perch to keep its balance. Do not dump the bird onto the perch. Keep your movements gentle, smooth, and confident. Again, as soon as it obeys, reward it with praise. These two commands are very simple and easy to learn, and they will keep you in control of your bird's movements. Most of my pet parrots will say "step up?" when they want me to pick them up and give them a cuddle. Once you begin working with your pet in a loving and consistent manner, you'll be surprised at how quickly it learns, and how eager it is to please you.

No parrot is born bad. A young bird learns how to behave from its parents and flock mates. I once allowed one of my breeding pairs of Senegal parrots to raise a chick to maturity. I have cameras in my aviary that are hooked to a television monitor in my kitchen, so I can watch "birdie TV" whenever I want. One afternoon, I watched as the mother bird and her newly weaned chick dozed next to each other on the perch. After a while, the baby looked over at his sleeping mother, reached down, and placed gentle pressure on her leg with his beak. Mom opened one eye and fixed the chick with a warning glare, and he promptly let go. A few minutes later, he repeated the action, but I could see he bit down slightly harder. This time the mother yanked her leg away, growled menacingly, and opened her beak in threat. The youngster scampered a few inches away, looking contrite. In a short while, mom once again dozed off, and I watched as the chick edged closer to her with a mischievous glint in his eyes. This time he leaned over and bit her *hard*. With an outraged shriek, the female knocked the chick completely off the perch onto the cage floor. While she sat on the perch above chattering and scolding, the father bird awoke from his nap at the other end of the cage. He immediately rushed to the cage floor, and began chasing the youngster about, growling and administering a few gentle warning nips. The chick rolled onto its back in submission, and after a stern glare, the father climbed up next to his mate to settle her down. After a few minutes, the youngster sheepishly climbed up onto the perch and snuggled between his parents, who both gently preened and smoothed his feathers. All was forgiv-

A Moluccan cockatoo practices the "step up" command from the back of a chair.

en, but it was quite clear that the baby had learned a valuable lesson: biting family members is not acceptable behavior, and it would not be tolerated.

SETTING LIMITS

Once you adopt a cockatoo into your household, it is up to you to teach the bird what is acceptable and what is not. The bird has no way of knowing that chewing holes in your new Italian leather sofa might displease you. Proper parrot training starts with you, the owner. You must first understand what is reasonable to expect from your bird, and what is not. When people contact me to buy a baby parrot, I always ask them what they're looking for in a pet bird. A surprising number of people believe that parrots are low maintenance, quiet pets. Nothing could be further from the truth. A cockatoo is the intellectual and emotional equivalent of a very bright and precocious human preschooler, except it's also equipped with wings, a massive, potentially destructive beak, and a more powerful set of lungs.

To begin, understand that parrots scream at times. For the most part, a very quiet parrot is probably a sick or depressed parrot. Even a well-behaved bird will likely greet sunrise and sunset with a few screeches, and it will have some exuberant moments during the day. It is not fair to punish them for this natural behavior. If you live in an apart-

Talk training may help channel a bird's energy away from such destructive habits as biting, screaming, and feather plucking.

A certain level of noise is completely natural for cockatoos, but excessive screaming may be a sign of frustration or loneliness.

chick constantly at first. At some point, real life intrudes and the family returns to work and school. At this point, the now very spoiled cockatoo begins to scream in outrage at the unfairness of it all. Soon, a family member rushes over to comfort it, and a habit is born. From the first moment you bring your new pet home, establish a schedule for time out of the cage and playtime, and stick with it as faithfully as possible. Once your bird learns that it can depend on a certain amount of quality time with the family each day, it will be more likely to play independently at other times.

If, despite a regular schedule, your cockatoo screams constantly for atten-ment with paper-thin walls, then a cockatoo might not be a suitable pet for you. On the other hand, mindless shrieking for hours on end is not acceptable, and it's okay to expect your bird to play quietly at times.

PROBLEM SCREAMING

Problem screaming is usually a learned behavior. In many cases, hand-reared baby cockatoos are never taught to amuse themselves and play independently. They're so darn cute, the breeder and then the new owner dote on them, petting and playing with the

Cockatoos love to be scratched and cuddled. Don't forget to save time for this necessary show of affection.

tion, carefully examine how you are reacting to it. Most cockatoos are "drama queens," and if you scream back at them or smack their cage with your hand, the bird will most likely enjoy the interaction, and be motivated to continue the negative behavior. Mikey, my Moluccan, is a perfect example of this personality type. When I got Mikey 15 years ago, I was new to birds and didn't have a clue about proper training. His incessant screaming made me crazy, and I'd often find myself standing in front of his cage, red-faced and angry, screaming back at him. When I did so, he'd bob and dance excitedly around the cage. As soon as I walked away, he'd start screaming again. It took me a while to realize that he thought he'd invented the perfect game: he'd scream, "Mommy" would come running and scream, he'd dance about, and I'd flail my arms in anger and frustration. He loved it! Soon, I began to say quietly but firmly "Mikey, no scream!" If he continued, I'd simply walk over, toss a cover over his cage, and leave the room. As soon as he settled down, I'd remove the cover and praise him lavishly. It took just a few days of this for him to learn that screaming made me go away, while being quiet brought love and attention. Now he's a perfect gentleman, at least most of the time. Please note that time-outs like this are only effective if you return to the bird after a few

Birds usually bite for a reason; perhaps your biter is frightened or trying to show dominance over you.

minutes and offer praise. Some people leave parrots covered for extended periods, or move the cage to a remote part of the house. This is cruel, and will only cause your pet to begin screaming even more out of frustration.

BITING AND DOMINANCE

Besides constant screaming, unprovoked biting is another bad habit that shouldn't be tolerated. However, there are many reasons why birds bite, and first you must decide what caused the incident. If your pet was frightened, hurt, or reacting to teasing, then biting is a natural defense and shouldn't be punished. If it's merely being a bully, then you have a behavioral problem. If

Height is an important factor in dominance issues; a bird that is allowed to ride on your shoulder or head will think that he is the "top bird."

you haven't yet clipped the bird's wings, it's not surprising that it bites. A free-flighted bird will likely have dominance issues with humans. Because it can fly and you can't, it will assume that it is the "alpha bird" and you are a subordinate flock member. This is a situation that usually leads to biting when the bird tries to get you to obey. Once its wings are clipped, the bird might stop biting without further incident.

If the biting continues, see if you can identify a common trigger. For example, does your pet bite you every time your spouse walks into the room? It might be jealousy. Try giving the bird extra attention and treats every time your spouse comes near, so that it

begins to associate his/her presence with good things. If it bites anyway, say "No!" in a firm voice and immediately return it to its cage. Does it bite when it's tired? Maybe you need to set an earlier birdie bedtime. If you are aware of your pet's body language, you can defuse many situations before a problem occurs. You must also be consistent with your corrections. If one family member allows the bird to bite

Though it can be caused by poor nutrition or allergies, feather-plucking is generally a sign of stress or emotional problems.

Trick training is an excellent way to focus your bird's energy on something productive and positive—and it's another way for you to spend time together.

without correction, it's a sure bet that it will continue to bite that person, despite your best efforts at breaking the habit. To properly train a parrot, you must immediately discipline bad behavior, and always remember to reward good behavior.

How do you discipline a parrot? That depends a great deal on the individual bird's personality. Some are so sensitive that a stern glance is punishment enough. Others will respond to a sharp, firm "No!" Outgoing, aggressive birds might need a time-out, where they're removed from the action and left to mull over their misdeeds. Again, never extend a time-out for longer than 10 to 15 minutes, or it

will only frustrate the bird and possibly increase the negative behavior. And never, ever hit your bird. Not only do you run the very real risk of injuring or even killing it, but also you will destroy its trust in you and teach it that violence is acceptable.

FEATHER PLUCKING

Feather plucking is perhaps the opposite of unprovoked biting. In this situation, instead of outward aggression, the cockatoo turns its emotions inward and begins plucking, chewing, or overpreening its own feathers. There are many causes of this disorder, and it's not always possible to break the habit once it begins. First of all, get the bird to an experienced avian vet as soon as the problem starts. Sometimes there's an underlying physical cause, like allergies, poor nutrition, infection, or parasites. If your pet gets a clean bill of health, then you'll need to start playing detective to determine the emotional cause. In cockatoos, boredom, stress, depression, and hormones (wanting to breed) all can play a role. Try to understand what your pet is feeling. If it appears bored, some new toys might be a quick fix, especially toys that have rope to preen and wood to chew. If it appears stressed, you might need to move its cage to a more suitable location, cut down on the noise level from children or other pets, and make sure the bird is getting enough sleep. In general, parrots

A Sulphur-crested cockatoo delights in learning to "wave hello" to its owner.

require about ten hours of sleep each night. If it seems depressed, maybe it's not getting enough love and attention. Cockatoos thrive on love, and a neglected bird will suffer greatly. Some mature birds get a little hormone rush occasionally, and might get a little nutty.

As you can see, there's no easy answer to the problem of feather-picking. I have seen cockatoos in perfect health, in wonderful homes filled with love, and with enough toys to keep a whole flock busy, and yet they still pluck. Often these owners are filled with guilt and will beg me to tell them what they're "doing wrong." If you've taken all the proper steps and your bird continues to pluck, you might have to ignore the problem and resolve to love them even though they're naked and ugly. Some vets will use sedating drugs, antidepressants, or plastic collars to thwart feather-pickers, but in my experience these should only be used in rare cases where the bird begins to damage its flesh and create a life-threatening situation. The plastic collars prevent normal preening, playing, and sleeping postures, and make the bird absolutely miserable. Drugs often create a zombie-like creature that's too wiped out to do anything normally; these drugs can also have a long-term effect on the liver and other organs. Some people have had good luck with homeopathic and herbal remedies, but

THE GUIDE TO OWNING A COCKATOO

Cockatoos must chew, so it's best to protect your furniture by providing your pet with suitable toys and objects to gnaw on.

use these only under the guidance of an experienced practitioner.

CHEWING

Another problem that cockatoo owners sometimes face is the bird's insatiable need to chew. One look at their massive beaks should leave no question about the evolutionary selection of these parrots: these guys are "born to chew," and they're not particularly fussy about how they satisfy that urge. This is really a problem that some cockatoo owners create for themselves through poor supervision. If you clip your pet's wings and never leave it unsupervised, then you won't have to deal with having a dining room set reduced to kindling wood. Always give your bird plenty of safe toys to exercise its beak. If you're tired of buying expensive bird toys only to see them destroyed in minutes, whole coconuts, chunks of untreated lumber, rolled up newspapers, and corrugated boxes are all inexpensive and a fun treat. I suggest you get a playstand that your pet can sit on when it's out of its cage, and equip it with plenty of "chewables." That way, the wooden trim around your windows might not look so tempting when you leave the room.

I've found that most behavioral problems are simply stages that a parrot goes through as it learns to live with its human flockmates. With a little gentle discipline and a lot of love, your new cockatoo should blossom into a wonderful companion that will fill your life with affection and fun.

Resources

AFA Watchbird
American Federation of Aviculture, Inc.
P.O. Box 56218
Phoenix, AZ 85079
www.afa.birds.org
   The AFA is a nonprofit organization dedicated to the promotion of aviculture and the conservation of avian wildlife through the encouragement of captive-breeding programs, scientific research, and the education of the general public. The AFA publishes a bi-monthly magazine called AFA Watchbird.

Association of Avian Veterinarians
P.O. Box 811720
Boca Raton, FL 33481
561-393-8901
www.aav.org
   AAV membership is comprised of veterinarians from private practice, zoos, universities and industry, veterinary educators, researchers and technicians, and veterinary students. Serves as resource for bird owners who are looking for certified avian veterinarians.

Bird Talk
Subscription Dept.
P.O. Box 57347
Boulder, CO 80323
www.animalnetwork.com
Bird Talk is a monthly magazine noted for its directory of avian breeders, as well as its informative articles and columns on health care, conservation, and behavior.

Bird Times
Pet Publishing, Inc.
7-L Dundas Circle
Greensboro, NC 27407
www.birdtimes.com
Bird Times is a source of entertaining and authoritative information about birds. Articles include bird breed profiles, medical reports, training advice, bird puzzles, and stories about special birds.

The Gabriel Foundation
P.O. Box 11477
Aspen, CO 81612
www.thegabrielfoundation.org
   The Gabriel Foundation is a nonprofit organization dedicated to promoting education, rescue, adoption, and sanctuary for parrots.

Midwest Avian Research Expo (MARE)
10430 Dewhurst Rd.
Elyria, OH 44036
www.mare-expo.org
   MARE is a nonprofit group dedicated to education and fundraising for avian research projects.

National Animal Poison Control Center/ASPCA
888-426-4435
900-680-0000
   In a life-and-death poisoning situation you can call this hotline for 24-hour emergency information. Please note that there is a charge for this service.

Index

Photo Credits

Larry Allan, 3, 16B, 44, 46, 48, 59, 60
Joan Balzarini, 7B, 9, 39, 41, 43, 51, 53, 61
Susan Chamberlain, 18
Isabelle Francais, 1, 10, 11B, 12, 15, 16T, 17, 22, 23, 25, 28, 30, 31T, 31B, 33, 35, 40, 56T, 57, 58T, 58B
Eric Ilasenko, 6, 14, 27
Robert Pearcy, 4, 37
Rafi Reyes, 5B, 7B, 13, 26, 34, 50
Peter Rimsa, 5T, 8, 20T, 20B, 21, 29, 36, 42, 45, 47, 54
Lara Stern, 19, 32, 49T, 52, 55
John Tyson, 11T, 24, 38, 49B, 56B